I0821032

THE 2000s

THROUGH THE DECADES

BY BETSY RATHBURN

eureka!

Eureka! books turn real stories into unforgettable experiences. This nonfiction imprint sparks curiosity, encourages critical thinking, and engages middle-grade readers. *Eureka!* books empower young minds to explore the stories of the real world, one fascinating fact at a time. Unravel the power of knowledge and lifelong learning with *Eureka!*

This edition first published in 2026 by Bellwether Media, Inc.

Library of Congress Cataloging-in-Publication Data

LC record for The 2000s available at: https://lccn.loc.gov/2025026509

Editor: Rebecca Sabelko Designer: Brittany McIntosh Series Designer: Andrea Schneider

Printed in the United States of America, North Mankato, MN.

TABLE OF CONTENTS

WELCOME TO THE 2000s!

One summer morning, a girl turns on her home computer. She opens *The Sims* to check on her characters and add decorations to their house. After a while, she closes the game and opens iTunes. She downloads songs to add to her iPod nano. Then, she signs on to AOL Instant Messenger. She chats with a friend about their plans to see a movie that evening.

The girl's brother asks if she wants to go outside. He skateboards while she rides her Razor scooter. They stay outside until it is time to go shopping. The family heads to the mall, where they pick out new clothes for school. They browse Hollister, Hot Topic, and Abercrombie & Fitch. When they are done shopping, the girl texts her friend on her Motorola Razr. They agree to meet at the movie theater. They decide to see the latest Harry Potter movie!

THE SIMS

IPOD NANO

MOTOROLA RAZR

HOT TOPIC
Razor scooter

WHAT HAPPENED IN THE 2000s?

At the start of the decade, many looked to the new **millennium** with hope for the future. Technological growth was speeding up, and opportunity came with it. In the 1990s, computers and the internet became more widespread, with more people logging in at work and at home every day. This led to even more growth in the 2000s. By the end of the decade, nearly 2 billion people worldwide had internet access. Personal blogging and social media let people connect with others around the world. The birth of smartphones helped people stay connected on the go.

The decade was also a time of conflict and uncertainty. Clashes in the Middle East during the 1990s set the stage for the years to come. After **terrorists** attacked the United States on September 11, 2001, the U.S. entered a period of tighter homeland security. A new law gave the government more power to spy on citizens. The country also entered wars in the Middle East that lasted the rest of the decade and beyond.

Near the end of the 2000s, a global **recession** brought economic crisis to much of the world. Many people in the U.S. lost their jobs or homes.

NEWS ARTICLE ABOUT THE MILLENNIUM

Y2K BUG

Before the new year, many people worried about a computer issue often called the Y2K, or millennium, bug. The concern had to do with how computers dealt with dates after 1999. Some people prepared for disaster. However, few issues arose.

HOW MUCH?

1 GALLON GAS
$1.51 (2000)
$2.35 (2009)

THE NEW YORK TIMES
(late edition)
$0.75 (2000) | $2.00 (2009)

MOVIE TICKET
$5.39 (2000)
$7.50 (2009)

HALF GALLON ICE CREAM
$3.32 (2000)
$4.44 (2009)

LOAF OF BREAD
$0.91 (2000)
$1.39 (2009)

1 GALLON MILK
$2.78 (2000)
$3.11 (2009)

2-LITER BOTTLE OF COKE
$1.07 (2000)
$1.37 (2009)

HISTORY

UNITED STATES HISTORY

On September 11, 2001, terrorists attacked the U.S. The U.S. soon declared war on Afghanistan in **retaliation**. The war on terrorism deepened in 2003 when the U.S. and other countries invaded Iraq. They overthrew the government of Saddam Hussein and searched for weapons of mass destruction. People criticized both the Iraq War and the war on terrorism. They opposed human rights violations in Afghanistan, Iraq, and at the U.S. military prison at Guantánamo Bay.

Several disasters marked the decade. In 2003, the space shuttle Columbia broke apart as it returned to Earth. Everyone on board died. In 2006, an explosion at the Sago Mine in West Virginia led to 12 deaths. However, journalists first reported that everyone lived. The disaster led to discussions of journalistic **integrity** and increased safety measures in mining.

SEPTEMBER 11, 2001 ATTACK

PROTEST AGAINST THE IRAQ WAR

SPACE SHUTTLE COLUMBIA

HURRICANE KATRINA

In 2005, Hurricane Katrina made landfall on the Gulf Coast of the U.S. Strong winds damaged homes and infrastructure. Important levees failed in New Orleans, Louisiana, causing much of the city to flood. The hurricane became the most expensive natural disaster in U.S. history. It is estimated that more than 1,800 people lost their lives and millions lost their homes.

THE GREAT RECESSION

In 2007, the Great Recession began. Many people lost their jobs, homes, and savings. This increased the wealth gap in the U.S. The recession ended in 2009, but many struggled to recover what they had lost.

VIRGINIA TECH SHOOTING

On April 16, 2007, a shooter at Virginia Polytechnic Institute and State University took the lives of 32 people and wounded 17 others. At the time, it was the deadliest mass shooting in U.S. history. It sparked discussions about gun control nationwide. Virginia tightened its laws around who could buy guns, but the shooting did not lead to any new federal laws.

candlelight vigil for the victims of the Virginia Tech shooting

UNITED STATES POLITICS

In 2000, Republican George W. Bush ran against Vice President Al Gore in a controversial presidential election. The race turned up no clear winner on election night. After multiple recounts and a legal battle, the U.S. Supreme Court declared Bush the winner.

A BIG LOSS

Gore won around 500,000 more votes than Bush, but he still lost the election. This was the first time this had happened in 112 years.

President George W. Bush

ELECTION SHOWDOWN: 2000 PRESIDENTIAL ELECTION

GORE (DEMOCRATIC)

BUSH (REPUBLICAN)

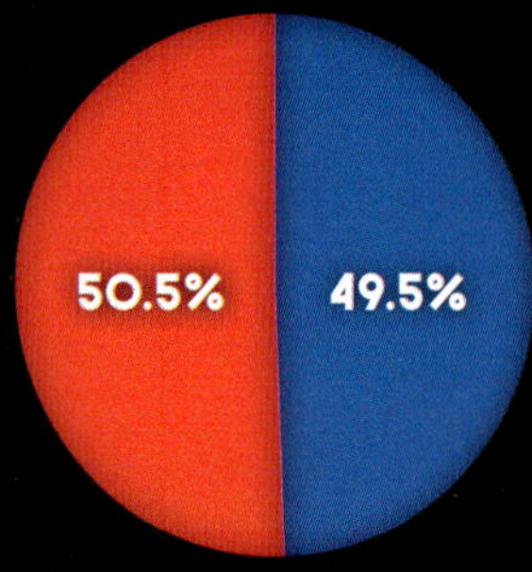

ELECTORAL VOTES

In 2001, President Bush withdrew from the **Kyoto Protocol**, saying it would harm the U.S. economy. In 2002, he signed the No Child Left Behind Act. Its goal was to give all students an equal chance to do well in school. Student test scores affected how much money schools received from the government. Many supported it at first, but others questioned its fairness.

In 2004, Bush was reelected. But his popularity had begun to decline. Democrats gained control of Congress during the 2006 midterm elections. Nancy Pelosi became the first female Speaker of the House. In 2005 and 2006, Bush appointed two U.S. Supreme Court justices. Rulings on the death penalty and gun rights followed.

In 2008, Barack Obama's policies for change won over voters. He became the country's first Black president. He signed laws to add jobs and protect fair pay.

VICE PRESIDENT AL GORE

SPEAKER OF THE HOUSE NANCY PELOSI

SUPREME COURT JUSTICE JOHN G. ROBERTS

President Barack Obama

SPOTLIGHT ON:

9/11 ATTACKS

On the morning of September 11, 2001, **hijackers** took control of four airplanes traveling from the East Coast to California. At 8:46 a.m., one of the planes crashed into the World Trade Center's North Tower in New York City. About 15 minutes later, a second plane hit the South Tower.

Soon, the third plane hit the Pentagon in Washington, D.C. Passengers on the fourth plane fought for control and crash-landed in Pennsylvania. All of the passengers on board each plane died instantly. People in the buildings also died. Both World Trade Center buildings eventually collapsed, killing and injuring many more people. Nearly 3,000 people lost their lives in the attacks that day.

A terrorist group called al-Qaeda was responsible for the attacks. The group's leader was Osama bin Laden. The U.S. government responded by declaring war on Afghanistan, where bin Laden had been granted **asylum**.

Americans immediately came together to mourn the attacks. The attacks also led to tighter airport security in the U.S. and around the world. The U.S. increased its **surveillance** of people suspected of being terrorists. This surveillance often targeted Muslim and Middle Eastern people, leading to increased **racism** and **hate crimes** against them.

ATTACK ON THE WORLD TRADE CENTER

ATTACK ON THE PENTAGON

9/11 MEMORIAL

WHO'S WHO?

GEORGE W. BUSH

ROLE:
President of the U.S. (2001–2009)

KNOWN FOR:
Leader of the U.S. who declared war on Afghanistan after the 9/11 attacks

OSAMA BIN LADEN

ROLE:
Leader of al-Qaeda (1988–2011)

KNOWN FOR:
Led al-Qaeda and organized the 9/11 attacks

WORLD HISTORY

Wars led by the U.S. affected many countries. Some, including the United Kingdom and Australia, sent troops to fight alongside American troops. In the Middle East, the invasion of Afghanistan ended **Taliban** rule until 2021. The Iraq War caused instability in Iraq and nearby countries. The 2003 capture and 2006 death of Iraqi leader Saddam Hussein stirred even more conflict.

Conflicts in Africa made the news, too. War in the Darfur region of Sudan broke out in 2003. Rebels protested the treatment of non-Arab people in Sudan by attacking a government base. The government brutally struck back, killing at least 200,000 people in a **genocide** by 2005. In Somalia, a civil war that began in the 1990s continued throughout the decade.

In 2002, an outbreak of the SARS virus led to over 900 deaths around the world. Scientists quickly developed treatment. The last known case was in 2004.

SADDAM HUSSEIN

SARS OUTBREAK

MONEY MATTERS

By 2002, the euro became the sole form of currency in 12 European countries. Each country switched from its own currency to the euro.

Hugo Chávez

THE IRAQ WAR

On March 19, 2003, the U.S. led an invasion of Iraq. Allied troops from several other countries joined in support. Leaders of these countries believed that Iraq hid weapons of mass destruction. They also wanted to end the brutal rule of Iraqi leader Saddam Hussein. He was captured that December, but no weapons were ever found.

POLITICAL CHANGES IN LATIN AMERICA

Latin America experienced many political changes in the 2000s. In 1998, Hugo Chávez was elected president in Venezuela. In the years that followed, many other progressive leaders came to power in Latin America. These leaders advocated for improving lives through access to better housing, improved education, and health care.

THE GAZA STRIP

In 2006, a group called Hamas won an election against the longstanding Fatah party in Palestine. This let Hamas take control of a Palestinian territory called the Gaza Strip. Palestine had been in conflict with Israel for many years. Israel believed the Hamas takeover was hostile toward Israel. It imposed a blockade on Gaza. The blockade restricted the movement of people and goods in and out of Gaza.

Palestinians protesting the blockade

SPOTLIGHT ON:

THE INDIAN OCEAN TSUNAMI

On December 26, 2004, there was a powerful earthquake under the ocean near Sumatra, an island in Indonesia. With a magnitude of 9.1, it was one of the biggest earthquakes ever recorded. The earthquake caused a series of waves called a tsunami. The waves traveled nearly 2,000 miles (3,219 kilometers) to the eastern coast of Africa.

The countries closest to where the earthquake began had little warning as the waves reached their shores. In some places, the waves were 30 feet (9 meters) tall. The tsunami killed around 228,000 people in 15 countries.

Problems emerged once the waves subsided. Roads, bridges, and buildings were washed away. Many people could not access food, water, or medical treatment, leading to more deaths. People lost their homes and jobs, making recovery difficult. Aid organizations worked for years to help with the recovery. Other organizations formed to create tsunami warning systems. They educate people about signs of a tsunami.

MAKING HEADLINES

"Quake, waves kill thousands"

—*Chicago Tribune*, December 27, 2004

"TSUNAMI KILLS THOUSANDS ACROSS NATIONS"

—*THE HINDU*, DECEMBER 27, 2004

TSUNAMI DESTRUCTION
IN INDIA
"Thousands Die as Quake-Spawned Waves Crash Onto Coastlines Across Southern Asia"
—The New York Times, December 27, 2004
aftermath of tsunami
in Indonesia

SOCIAL CHANGES

Public approval of **LGBTQ+** rights grew in the 2000s. In 2004, Massachusetts became the first state to legalize same-sex marriage. Other states followed, but not everyone supported the change. President Bush supported a nationwide ban on same-sex marriage. However, the federal government did not rule on the issue during the decade.

Crime rates dropped steadily during the decade. By 2009, the rate of violent crime had reached its lowest point since 1973. Still, the number of mass shootings slowly rose. This sparked debate around gun control. By 2005, just over half of Americans supported stricter gun laws. That number shrank to under half by 2010. In 2008, the *District of Columbia v. Heller* Supreme Court case guaranteed the right to possess guns.

Immigration grew in the U.S. during the 2000s, reaching its peak in 2007. By the end of the decade, the nation was home to a record 40 million immigrants. After the 9/11 attacks, some Americans worried about how immigration affected national security. The U.S. government set more limits on who could enter the country. Still, most Americans believed immigration was good for the country.

IMMIGRANT RIGHTS PROTESTS

In December 2005, the House of Representatives passed a bill called the Border Protection, Antiterrorism, and Illegal Immigration Control Act. Many people argued this bill violated human rights. Between February and May 2006, around six million people in cities across the nation protested the bill. The Senate did not pass the bill. Immigration legislation continued to surface in Congress for many years. It continues to be a major political topic today.

SAME-SEX MARRIAGE LEGALIZED IN MASSACHUSETTS

DICK HELLER, DISTRICT OF COLUMBIA V. HELLER

BORDER PATROL

SCIENCE AND TECHNOLOGY

TECHNOLOGICAL ADVANCEMENTS

Home computers became more common in the 2000s. Just over half of people in the U.S. used the internet in 2000. By 2010, that number rose to more than 7 out of 10. Instant messaging and chat rooms were popular ways to communicate online. Later, social media platforms such as Facebook took over. In 2005, YouTube was launched. Two years later, Netflix began offering TV shows and movies to stream.

People used new devices on the go. In 2001, Apple released the first iPod. The device's simple, user-friendly design made it a huge success. People used iTunes to download digital music for their iPods. E-reader devices also took off, letting people easily download digital books. The Sony Reader was released in 2006. The Amazon Kindle came out the next year.

IPHONE

WHAT IS IT?:
A mobile smartphone that combined a digital camera and music player and had the ability to access the internet

INVENTOR:
Apple

YEAR INVENTED:
2007

EFFECT ON DAILY LIFE:
Gave people access to the internet on the go and allowed them to constantly stay connected using social media and text messaging

Mobile phone use grew over the decade. In 2003, the Nokia 1100 was released. More than 250 million sold, making it the best-selling cell phone ever. Use of smartphones grew. The first iPhone was released in 2007. Its touch screen and App Store made it unique among smartphones at the time.

MILLIONS OF MESSAGES

As more people used mobile phones, text messaging became more popular. In 2005, people sent 81 billion text messages per day in the U.S. By 2010, more than 2 trillion were sent per day!

ADVANCEMENTS IN SCIENCE AND MEDICINE

One important advancement of the 2000s built on work that started in the 1990s. The Human Genome Project finished in 2003. This project mapped human **DNA**. The work helped doctors treat diseases and improve medications. Scientists also mapped DNA for other life during the decade, including chimpanzees and several plants.

Debate rose around the use of human **stem cells** in scientific research. The stem cells could help treat diseases. But getting stem cells meant destroying human **embryos**. In 2001, President Bush limited government money for stem cell research. Later, scientists discovered a new way to get stem cells, and President Obama loosened the rules. Scientists now study the use of stem cells to fight cancer, diabetes, and other diseases.

The decade had exciting advances in physics, too. Use of the Large Hadron Collider began in 2008. This machine speeds up particles and encourages them to crash together. Scientists study the matter created from crashes. It helps them explore theories of physics.

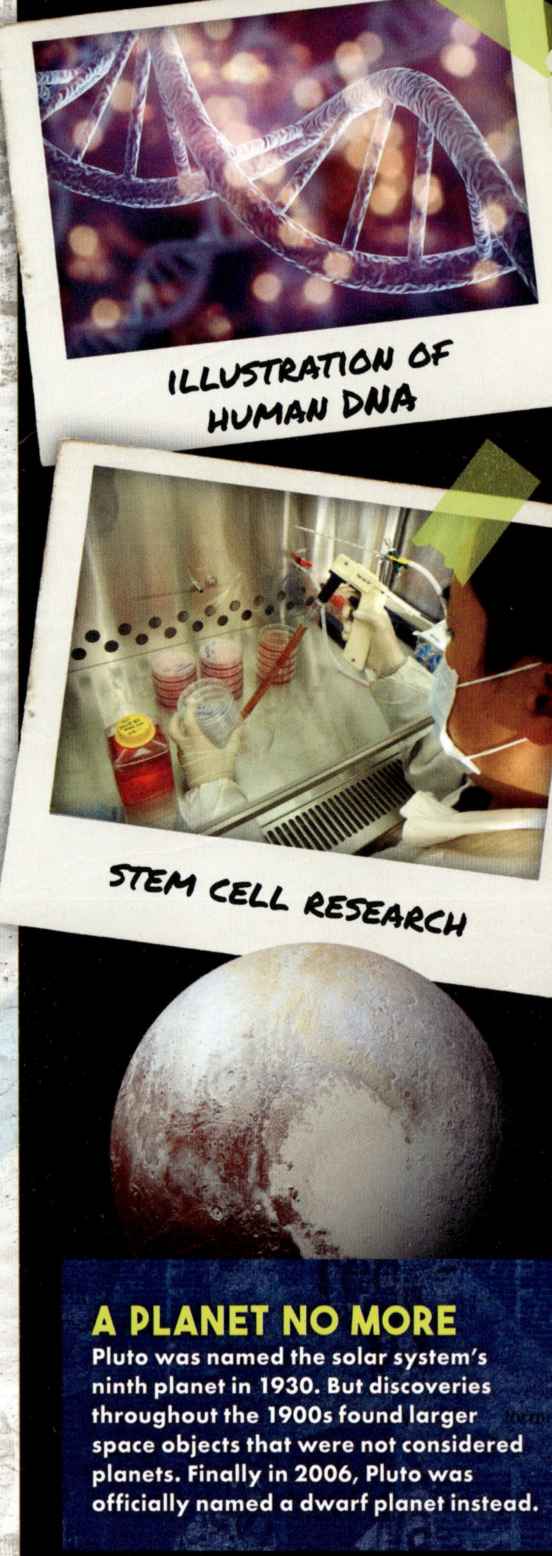

ILLUSTRATION OF HUMAN DNA

STEM CELL RESEARCH

A PLANET NO MORE

Pluto was named the solar system's ninth planet in 1930. But discoveries throughout the 1900s found larger space objects that were not considered planets. Finally in 2006, Pluto was officially named a dwarf planet instead.

Space science also advanced. In 2001, the WMAP satellite was launched to measure radiation in space. Its discoveries were used to determine the universe's age, history, and matter.

DAILY LIFE

LIFE IN THE 2000s

Urban areas in the U.S. grew during the 2000s. Many young adults moved to cities after college. Meanwhile, suburbs also grew. This continued a trend that had started decades earlier. Large trucks such as the Ford F-Series were among the most popular vehicles. But interest in electric cars slowly grew. In 2008, the first battery-powered Tesla was released.

The Great Recession caused instability for many people. The middle class shrank. Many people lost their jobs and struggled to find more work. Some lost their homes. The effect was greater for Black and Latino people. These groups were more likely to experience hardship, and it was more difficult for them to recover. **Multigenerational** households increased, especially during and after the recession. Many people lived with extended family.

Technology also changed daily life. Online shopping gained popularity, with retailers such as Amazon making it easy to buy online. More people used the internet to connect and search. The internet was also used for fun. Kids spent less time outside than previous decades. They played video games online or used social media to talk to friends.

SUBURB

FORD F-150

AMAZON WEBSITE

2000s SLANG

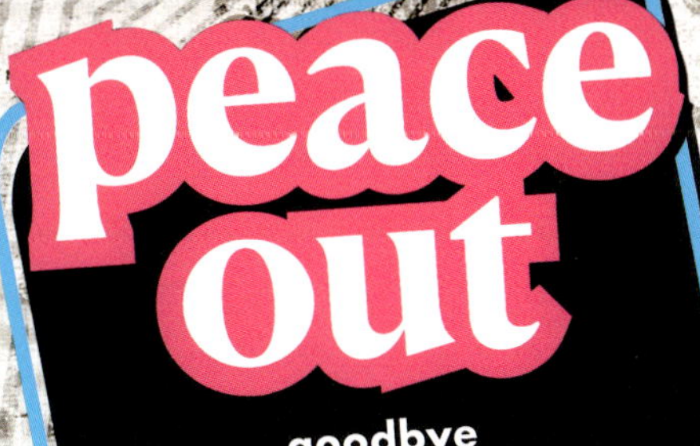

epic fail

a big failure, usually public

FASHION TRENDS

futuristic style

Futuristic clothing hit runways early in the decade. Many designs included metallic fabric, shiny leather, and the color black. Soon, more casual clothing came into style. Velour tracksuits were popular. They were often bright colors and paired with UGG boots. Trucker hats, especially those made by Von Dutch, topped off many outfits.

Low-rise flare jeans and miniskirts were popular in the early 2000s. They were often paired with cropped shirts. Polo shirts with popped collars and puka shell necklaces were trendy with both men and women. Men combined them with baggy cargo shorts. The boho trend of the mid-2000s led to the popularity of long, flowing layers. Maxi skirts and peasant tops became popular. These were sometimes worn over jeans. By the end of the decade, skinny jeans were more common. These were often paired with ballet flats and peplum tops.

Some fashion trends were inspired by music. Fans of pop-punk music wore skinny jeans, hooded sweatshirts, and Converse sneakers. Chunky skateboarding sneakers were also popular. Emo fans often wore black skinny jeans, studded belts, and band T-shirts. Choppy hairstyles with side-swept bangs accompanied this look. Hip-hop fans chose baggy clothes, including jeans, sports jerseys, and puffer jackets.

UGG boots

WHEELS ON HEELS

Heelys were a popular shoe in the 2000s. They came with wheels in their soles!

PUKA SHELL NECKLACE

VELOUR TRACKSUIT

EMO FASHION

PRODUCTS AND TOYS

Many popular toys in the 2000s were centered around technology. Games like Scene It? took advantage of the emerging popularity of DVD players. Video game consoles and robotic pets were also popular. Still, many of the most popular toys were played outside and away from screens.

BRATZ

In 2001, the first Bratz dolls were released, creating stiff competition for Barbie for the first time. The dolls have large eyes and pouty lips. At the time, their skin tones included more diversity than the Barbie brand. Their fashion mirrors real-world trends. By 2005, worldwide sales reached $2 billion.

SILLY BANDZ

Inspired by yellow Livestrong bracelets that were popular in the early 2000s, Robert Croak released Silly Bandz in 2008. These silicone bracelets come in hundreds of shapes, including animals, foods, and holiday items. They quickly became popular around the world. It was a multimillion-dollar fad that is gaining popularity again today!

RAZOR SCOOTERS

Razor scooters quickly became popular when they were released in 2000. More than 5 million sold in the first six months! The scooters are made of aluminum and can be folded in half. Riders have a choice of colors for their handles and wheels. Kids and adults alike enjoyed riding their scooters and trying new tricks.

Poo-Chi robotic dog

BEYBLADES

Based on a popular manga, Beyblades became a craze in the early 2000s. These spinning tops are used to battle. Opponents spin their tops and drop them into the same space. Players get points if their opponent's Beyblade goes out of the space, breaks apart, or stops spinning. Different types of Beyblades give battlers different advantages.

ROBOTIC PETS

The Poo-Chi robotic dog was released in 2000. More than 10 million sold in its first year. Tekno the Robotic Puppy and iDog were other popular robotic dog toys. The FurReal Friends robotic cat came out in 2002. The Zhu Zhu Pet was released in 2009. This furry robotic hamster had wheels to race across the floor.

Tony Hawk's Pro Skater 2

SKATEBOARDING

Skateboarding was wildly popular in the 2000s. Skateboarding video games such as the Tony Hawk's Pro Skater series, which began in 1999, grew in popularity with several new releases. Tech Decks were popular skateboarding toys. People used their fingers to ride miniature skateboards and do tricks on everyday objects.

VIDEO GAMES

The first Xbox was released in 2001. In 2005, the next generation, the Xbox 360, was released. The PlayStation 2 was released in 2000. More than 160 million sold, making it the best-selling console ever. In 2001, Nintendo's GameCube was unsuccessful compared to past consoles. Nintendo sales improved in 2006 with the release of the Wii.

ARTS AND ENTERTAINMENT

PUBLICATIONS

The 2000s brought change to how books were sold. At the start of the decade, Barnes & Noble was the top bookstore chain in the U.S. But growing online retailers meant more people began to buy books online. Amazon became the top online bookseller, drawing shoppers with its huge selection of millions of books.

Although most books were printed throughout the decade, buzz around e-books began around 2000. But e-books were still uncommon, and affordable e-readers were not available. In 2007, Amazon released the Kindle e-reader. It was not the first e-reader on the market, but it got people excited about reading digital books. The Kindle sold out within hours. Amazon offered a selection of 90,000 e-books for the device. In 2009, the company released new models. They sold even more than the original.

READING REC

TITLE:
THE HUNGER GAMES

AUTHOR:
Suzanne Collins

YEAR PUBLISHED:
2008

SUMMARY:
Katniss Everdeen represents her community in an event called the Hunger Games, in which contestants fight to be the sole survivor.

YA BESTSELLERS

Young adult (YA) fiction boomed in the 2000s. YA books such as 2003's *The Curious Incident of the Dog in the Night-Time* and 2007's *The Absolutely True Diary of a Part-Time Indian* won important awards. YA series also sold well. The Hunger Games, a dystopian series started in 2008, sold millions of copies.

MAGAZINES

Many magazines were popular among teens in the 2000s. *Teen People* included stories about celebrities. *Seventeen* and *CosmoGirl* featured articles about fashion, true stories from readers, and more. *Sports Illustrated* was popular among sports fans. Gamers enjoyed *Nintendo Power*. As the internet grew, many magazines focused on digital formats over print.

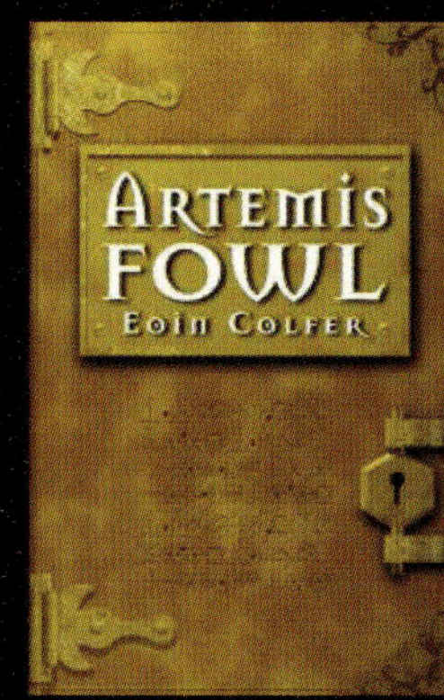

FANTASY SERIES

Starting in 1997 with the Harry Potter series, fantasy books gained ground in the 2000s. In 2007, *Harry Potter and the Deathly Hallows* became the fastest-selling book of all time. Harry Potter led to a rise in other YA fantasy series, including the Artemis Fowl, Percy Jackson, and Twilight series.

ON THE INTERNET

Online entertainment grew throughout the decade. Neopets let users care for virtual pets. Club Penguin and Webkinz were popular places to play games. People used GeoCities to create personal websites about their lives. Blogging platforms like LiveJournal made it even easier to share. In 2003, MySpace opened. Other social media platforms followed, including Facebook in 2004 and YouTube in 2005.

SELF-PUBLISHING

Easy-to-access publishing technology made it possible for authors to release books on their own. Starting in 2007, Amazon had a service to print books on demand. Books were not printed until someone ordered one. With the release of the Kindle, writers could also release their books digitally.

MOVIES

The 2000s was a decade of major blockbuster hits. The most popular films were those based on existing franchises, including books, comics, and even theme park rides. Advances in technology allowed many movies to use computer-generated imagery (CGI). **Motion capture** technology grew throughout the decade. Some movies also used 3D technology, including 2009's *Avatar*. It became the biggest blockbuster hit of all time. Many movies were released in IMAX during the 2000s, which further enhanced the moviegoing experience.

VHS tapes for home movie viewing gave way to DVDs. DVD sales were higher than VHS for the first time in 2003. In 2006, the first movies on Blu-Ray were released. This format had better quality and quickly replaced DVDs.

TEEN MOVIES

Released in 2004, *Mean Girls* is still hailed as one of the best teen movies of the decade. This movie tells the story of a group of popular girls. Teen movies featuring quirky characters, such as *Napoleon Dynamite* and *Juno*, won many fans. Musical dramas such as *Drumline* and *Stomp the Yard* were also popular.

Mean Girls

AT THE BOX OFFICE

TOP-GROSSING FILMS OF THE 2000s

- *Avatar* (2009)
- *The Lord of the Rings: The Return of the King* (2003)
- *Pirates of the Caribbean: Dead Man's Chest* (2006)
- *Harry Potter and the Sorcerer's Stone* (2001)
- *The Dark Knight* (2008)
- *Pirates of the Caribbean: At World's End* (2007)
- *Harry Potter and the Order of the Phoenix* (2007)
- *Finding Nemo* (2003)
- *The Lord of the Rings: The Two Towers* (2002)
- *Harry Potter and the Half-Blood Prince* (2009)

Harry Potter and the Sorcerer's Stone

COMPUTER ANIMATION

After growth in the 1990s, computer animation took off in the 2000s. In 2001, *Shrek* earned nearly $500 million at the box office. The movie influenced a shift from 2D animation to computer animation. Other popular computer-animated movies of the decade include *Finding Nemo*, *The Incredibles*, and *Cars*.

THE LORD OF THE RINGS

The Lord of the Rings trilogy began in 2001. The three films used groundbreaking digital technology. Motion capture helped create iconic characters such as Gollum. CGI was used to make monsters such as Shelob. CGI was paired with artificial intelligence to create huge battles.

Gollum

Jack Sparrow

PIRATES OF THE CARIBBEAN

Based on a ride at Disney theme parks, the Pirates of the Caribbean series delighted audiences. The swashbuckling story brought action and comedy to movie screens. The first three movies earned more than $1 billion from ticket sales.

SUPERHEROES ON FILM

Movies based on superhero comic books were popular in the 2000s. A Spider-Man trilogy starring Tobey Maguire was popular. Batman was also popular, with 2005's *Batman Begins* drawing big audiences. Its sequel, *The Dark Knight*, was released in 2008 to critical acclaim. *Iron Man* and *The Incredible Hulk* were other popular superhero films released in 2008.

FIRST OF ITS KIND

The 2004 movie *The Polar Express* was the first full-length movie to be made entirely using motion capture.

Spider-Man

TELEVISION

Television technology changed in the 2000s. Early in the decade, large, boxy TVs dominated the market. By 2005, the first flat-screen TVs were released. They were very expensive. Prices dropped as the new technology became more common.

High-definition (HD) TV took over during the 2000s. At first, few shows were broadcast in HD. This changed as more people purchased HD TVs. The switch from analog to digital TV in 2009 made more channels available with clearer pictures.

What people watched also changed. Many refer to the 2000s as the Golden Age of Television. Popular, high-quality shows were produced, especially on cable channels. Lower budget reality TV shows also became commonplace.

Survivor

REALITY TV

In 2000, *Survivor* set the stage for an explosion in reality TV. In 2002, *American Idol* became a phenomenon. Viewers voted on the next music superstar. The 2002 show *The Osbournes* let viewers watch celebrities' daily lives, paving the way for 2007's *Keeping Up with the Kardashians*. Other top reality shows included *Big Brother* and *Dancing with the Stars*.

Grey's Anatomy

POPULAR DRAMAS

ABC's medical drama *Grey's Anatomy* began in 2005 and continued into the 2020s. *Lost*, first aired in 2004, was another top ABC show that captivated audiences. On cable, the crime drama *The Sopranos* influenced many 2000s TV shows, leading to more dramas with complex plots. *The Wire*, started in 2002, explored politics and society. It is often considered the best TV show of the decade.

The Office (U.S.)

SITCOMS

In 2001, *The Office* first aired in the United Kingdom. Four years later, an American version debuted. Both shows influenced later workplace comedies such as 2009's *Parks and Recreation*. Beginning in 2007, *The Big Bang Theory* was a top sitcom, making science fun and approachable for many viewers. *The Bernie Mac Show* and *Everybody Hates Chris* were popular Black sitcoms.

CARTOONS

Kids had several networks to choose from to watch cartoons in the 2000s. Premiering in 1999, Nickelodeon's *SpongeBob SquarePants* was a cartoon phenomenon during the 2000s. Kids and adults alike were amused by the show's humor. In 2001, Disney aired *The Proud Family*. On Cartoon Network, *Teen Titans* was a popular superhero show.

Spongebob Squarepants

That's So Raven

TV FOR TEENS

Shows made for teens were immensely popular. *The O.C.* gained many fans. It followed a group of wealthy teenagers in California. *Gossip Girl* also followed wealthy teenagers. Both shows influenced fashion and music among teens. *That's So Raven* on the Disney Channel was about a teen who could see into the future.

MUSIC

The 2000s saw rapid changes in how people listened to music. When the decade started, compact discs were the main way to listen to music at home. This began to change when the first iPod was released in 2001. People could buy and download music from services such as iTunes and load it onto their devices.

Hip-hop was the top genre. Songs by Nelly, Outkast, Jay-Z, and 50 Cent topped the music charts. The rapper Eminem was the best-selling artist of the decade. Pop artists that began in the 1990s continued selling well, including the Backstreet Boys and Britney Spears. Meanwhile, new pop stars began to emerge. Country and rock also enjoyed popularity in the 2000s.

COUNTRY

An upswing in the popularity of country music began in the 2000s. New artists such as Miranda Lambert, Luke Bryan, and Blake Shelton recorded popular hits. *American Idol* fans voted country singer Carrie Underwood as the show's winner in 2005. In 2006, Taylor Swift's first album brought new fans to the country genre.

Taylor Swift

2000s PLAYLIST

- ***Poker Face***
  Lady Gaga (2008)
- ***Empire State of Mind***
  Jay-Z feat. Alicia Keys (2009)
- ***I Gotta Feeling***
  The Black Eyed Peas (2009)
- ***Hey Ya!***
  Outkast (2003)
- ***Umbrella***
  Rihanna feat. Jay-Z (2007)
- ***Crazy in Love***
  Beyoncé feat. Jay-Z (2003)
- ***Sk8er Boi***
  Avril Lavigne (2002)
- ***Welcome to the Black Parade***
  My Chemical Romance (2006)
- ***One More Time***
  Daft Punk (2000)
- ***Our Song***
  Taylor Swift (2006)
- ***Chicken Fried***
  Zac Brown Band (2005)

Beyoncé

ELECTRONIC

Technology made it easier for artists to make new kinds of electronic music, pushing the genre to the mainstream. By the end of the decade, established artists such as Daft Punk and Tiësto drew huge crowds. New forms of electronic music emerged, too. Dubstep, with its heavy drums and bass, began in the United Kingdom.

Daft Punk

POP

Pop in the 2000s was often influenced by hip-hop and dance music. Beyoncé emerged as a solo artist. Her first number one song, "Crazy in Love," launched her into superstardom. Justin Timberlake started his solo career, with his first album peaking near the top of charts. Rihanna and Lady Gaga also got their starts during the decade.

ROCK

Coldplay and Nickelback were successful rock bands during the 2000s. Pop-punk bands Blink-182 and Green Day saw huge success. Emo music focused on emotional themes. By the mid-2000s, Fall Out Boy and My Chemical Romance were among the top bands in this genre. Linkin Park was a favorite of alternative rock fans. Indie rock bands such as the White Stripes were popular with fans and critics.

HIP-HOP

During this time, many of hip-hop's top hits focused on themes of living a wealthy, flashy lifestyle. Artists such as Jay-Z, 50 Cent, and the Black Eyed Peas released popular songs. Missy Elliott won multiple Grammys for best rap solo performance. Artists such as Outkast and Lupe Fiasco drew in listeners with lyrics full of political and social commentary.

The Black Eyed Peas

Fall Out Boy

U.S. SPORTS

In the 2000s, U.S. sports fans witnessed many memorable moments. In baseball, the Boston Red Sox won the 2004 World Series, their first in 86 years. Many tuned in to the Super Bowl, too. The Rams, Ravens, Patriots, and Buccaneers all achieved their first Super Bowl wins.

After the Women's National Basketball Association (WNBA) began in the 1990s, star players began to emerge. In 2002, Lisa Leslie was the first WNBA player to dunk a basketball during a game. National Basketball Association (NBA) superstar Michael Jordan retired in 2003. That same year, LeBron James began his rise as a top player. Still, NBA viewership declined over the decade. More games began airing on cable. This made it more difficult for people to watch.

MVP

NAME:
TOM BRADY

SPORT:
Football

YEARS PLAYED:
2000 to 2023

TEAMS:
New England Patriots, Tampa Bay Buccaneers

KNOWN FOR:
Considered one of the best quarterbacks to ever play football, Brady led the New England Patriots to Super Bowl wins in 2002, 2004, and 2005.

Jeff Gordon

NASCAR

NASCAR saw a rise in popularity beginning in the 1990s, with popular drivers such as Jeff Gordon winning many fans. Millions of viewers began tuning in to watch races, and NASCAR's popularity peaked in 2005. Tragedy also struck. In 2001, legendary driver Dale Earnhardt passed away in a crash during the Daytona 500.

BASEBALL

Major League Baseball (MLB) faced controversy in the 2000s. Popular players were suspected or confirmed to be using steroids that helped them play better. Though steroids had been banned since the early 1990s, MLB did not start testing players until 2003. Starting in 2005, players who tested positive could be banned from baseball.

MALICE AT THE PALACE

In 2004, an NBA game between the Detroit Pistons and the Indiana Pacers led to a shocking brawl now known as Malice at the Palace. Both players and audience members were involved in the fight. The chaos led to arrests and legal issues. It also led to public disapproval of the NBA. The league changed its rules for players and events.

HOCKEY LOCKOUT

Players in the National Hockey League (NHL) refused to play for 10 months during the 2004–2005 season. They protested changes that would limit their pay. Once hockey started again the next season, fewer viewers than ever before were interested. However, exciting 2009 Stanley Cup games between the Pittsburgh Penguins and the Detroit Red Wings helped draw in more fans.

2009 Stanley Cup Final

GLOBAL SPORTS

International sports also saw excitement in the 2000s. The Olympics saw record-breaking performances in swimming, running, and more. New sports were added to the Games, including taekwondo, triathlon, trampoline, and BMX racing. Women's wrestling was added in 2004.

In soccer, top players such as Cristiano Ronaldo and Lionel Messi each began their rise to superstardom. The first FIFA World Cup of the new millennium was held in 2002. Brazil took the first victory of the decade. Wins for Italy in 2006 and Spain in 2010 followed. The Women's World Cup was held in 2003. Germany won against Sweden in the final. At the next Women's World Cup in 2007, Germany took the trophy again.

OLYMPICS OF THE 2000s

Lionel Messi

Cristiano Ronaldo

TENNIS STARS

Many famous tennis players found their first major success on the court in the 2000s. Roger Federer won his first Grand Slam title at Wimbledon in 2003. He went on to win 14 more titles during the decade. Rafael Nadal also rose to stardom, winning 6 Grand Slam titles. Serena Williams dominated women's tennis, winning 10 of her 23 Grand Slam singles titles between 2000 and 2009.

Serena Williams

RONALDO VS. MESSI

In 2002, Portuguese player Cristiano Ronaldo began his professional career with Sporting Lisbon, quickly moving to Manchester United in 2003. Ronaldo is often compared to Lionel Messi, an Argentinian player who debuted with Barcelona in 2004. Both players set records and led their teams to many titles over the decade.

THE WORLD'S FASTEST MAN

Jamaican runner Usain Bolt raced onto the Olympic stage in 2004. He came short of winning a medal. Four years later, he broke the world record in the 100 meters. He then won gold medals in every event he raced in at the 2008 Olympic games. In 2009, he broke his 100-meter record with a time of 9.58 seconds. The record still stands today!

SWIMMING TO THE GOLD

At the 2004 Olympic Games, U.S. swimmer Michael Phelps swam his way to six gold and two bronze medals. He also set new Olympic and world records in several events. At the next Olympic games in 2008, Phelps broke his own records. He took home eight gold medals, setting the record for most gold medals won at a single Olympic Games.

TIMELINE

JANUARY 1, 2000
The Y2K Bug does no damage to global computer systems

OCTOBER 26, 2001
The USA PATRIOT Act is signed into law

SEPTEMBER 11, 2001
Terrorists use airplanes to attack the World Trade Center and the Pentagon

JUNE 11, 2002
American Idol airs for the first time

OCTOBER 23, 2001
Apple releases the first iPod

MARCH 19, 2003
The U.S. invades Iraq

NOVEMBER 15, 2001
Microsoft releases the first Xbox

DECEMBER 12, 2000
George W. Bush is named the winner of the 2000 presidential election

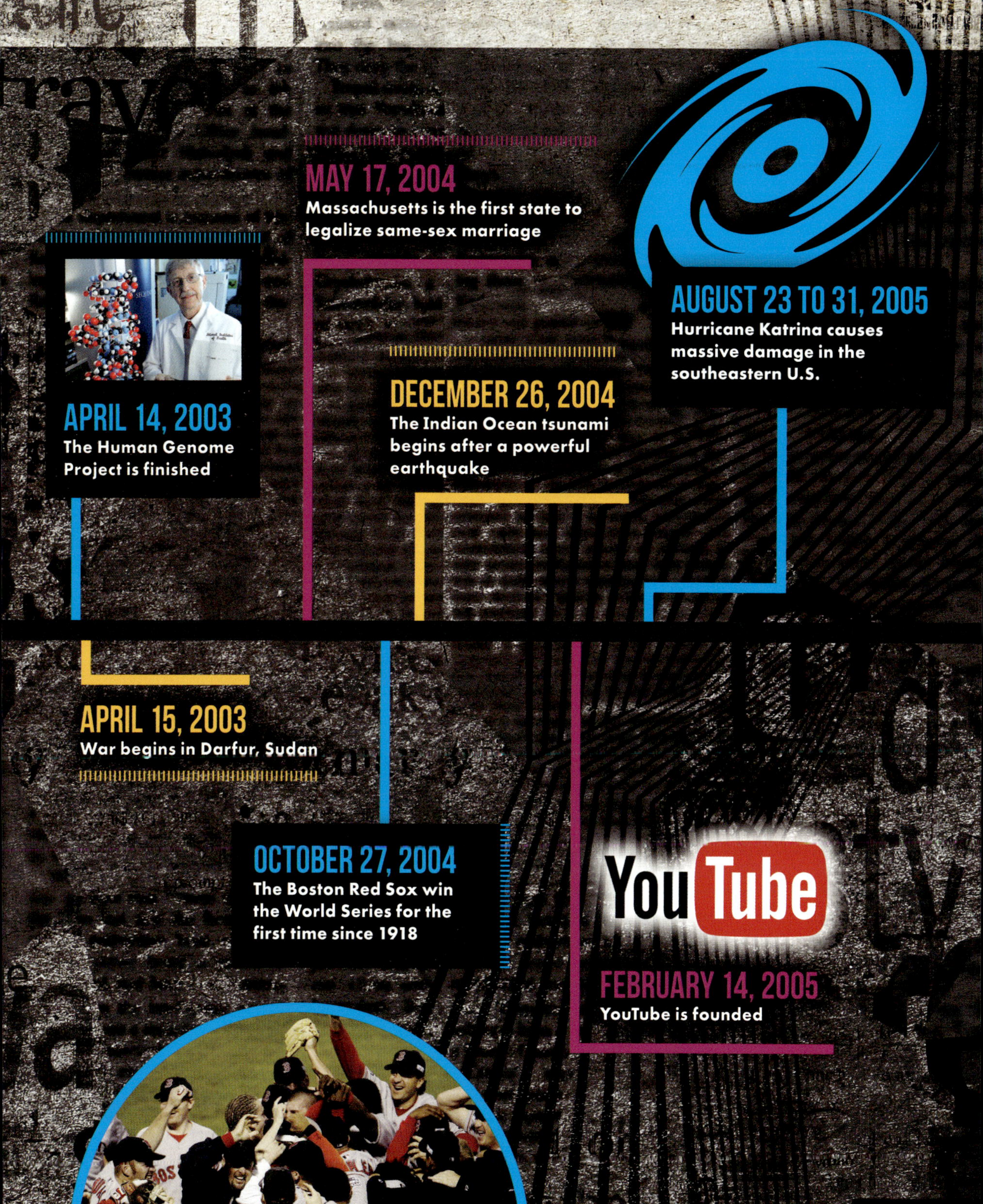
MAY 17, 2004
Massachusetts is the first state to legalize same-sex marriage
AUGUST 23 TO 31, 2005
Hurricane Katrina causes massive damage in the southeastern U.S.
APRIL 14, 2003
The Human Genome Project is finished
DECEMBER 26, 2004
The Indian Ocean tsunami begins after a powerful earthquake
APRIL 15, 2003
War begins in Darfur, Sudan
OCTOBER 27, 2004
The Boston Red Sox win the World Series for the first time since 1918
YouTube
FEBRUARY 14, 2005
YouTube is founded

JANUARY 25, 2006
Hamas wins an election in Palestine, leading to conflict with Israel and an eventual blockade of the Gaza Strip

AUGUST 24, 2006
Pluto is reclassified from planet to dwarf planet

NOVEMBER 19, 2006
The Nintendo Wii is released in North America

NOVEMBER 19, 2007
Amazon releases the first Kindle e-reader

JULY 20, 2006
War breaks out in Somalia

OCTOBER 24, 2006
Taylor Swift releases her first album

JUNE 29, 2007
Apple releases the first iPhone

DECEMBER 2007
The financial crisis known as the Great Recession begins

Avatar

JUNE 26, 2008
District of Columbia v. Heller upholds the right of U.S. citizens to possess firearms

AUGUST 17, 2008
Michael Phelps wins his record-setting eighth gold medal of the 2008 Summer Olympic Games

SEPTEMBER 10, 2008
Use of the Large Hadron Collider begins

NOVEMBER 4, 2008
Barack Obama is elected president of the U.S.

MARCH 9, 2009
President Obama removes restrictions on stem cell research

AUGUST 16, 2009
Usain Bolt sets the world record for the 100-meter dash with a time of 9.58 seconds

DECEMBER 18, 2009
Avatar, the top-earning movie of all time, is released

GLOSSARY

artificial intelligence—a computer's ability to do things a human mind can do

asylum—protection given by a nation to a person who has left their native country because of danger there

blockade—the act of closing a place to prevent goods or people from entering or leaving

diversity—having a variety of people or things from many different backgrounds

DNA—a substance that carries information about the makeup of a living thing

dystopian—related to a fictional society where there is a lot of injustice

embryos—animals that are just starting to develop

generation—a group of objects or beings that are created or formed around the same time

genocide—deliberate and systematic destruction of racial, political, or cultural groups

hate crimes—crimes against people based on their race, ethnicity, religion, gender, sexual orientation, or abilities

hijackers—people who take control of a vehicle

immigration—the act of moving to a new country

infrastructure—the structures that are needed for society to function; infrastructure includes buildings, roads, bridges, and power lines.

integrity—honesty and sincerity

Kyoto Protocol—an international agreement adopted in 1997 in which countries agreed to reduce greenhouse gas emissions to slow climate change

levees—structures built around rivers to prevent water from overflowing

LGBTQ+—a community of people who identify as something other than heterosexual or the gender they were assigned at birth; LGBTQ+ stands for Lesbian, Gay, Bisexual, Transgender, Queer, and other identities.

millennium—a period of a thousand years

motion capture—a technology that matches human movement to computer-generated characters

multigenerational—relating to more than one generation

progressive—interested in new ideas or ways of doing things

racism—the belief that race is a fundamental part of human traits and that certain races are superior to others

recession—a period of decline in economic activity, employment, and production that lasts more than a few months

retaliation—the act of striking back after an attack

stem cells—simple cells that can become cells with a special function

surveillance—the act of keeping a close watch on someone or something

Taliban—a religious and political group in Afghanistan that is known for its support of terrorism

terrorists—people who use violence and fear to try to control others

wealth gap—the unequal distribution of money between different groups of people

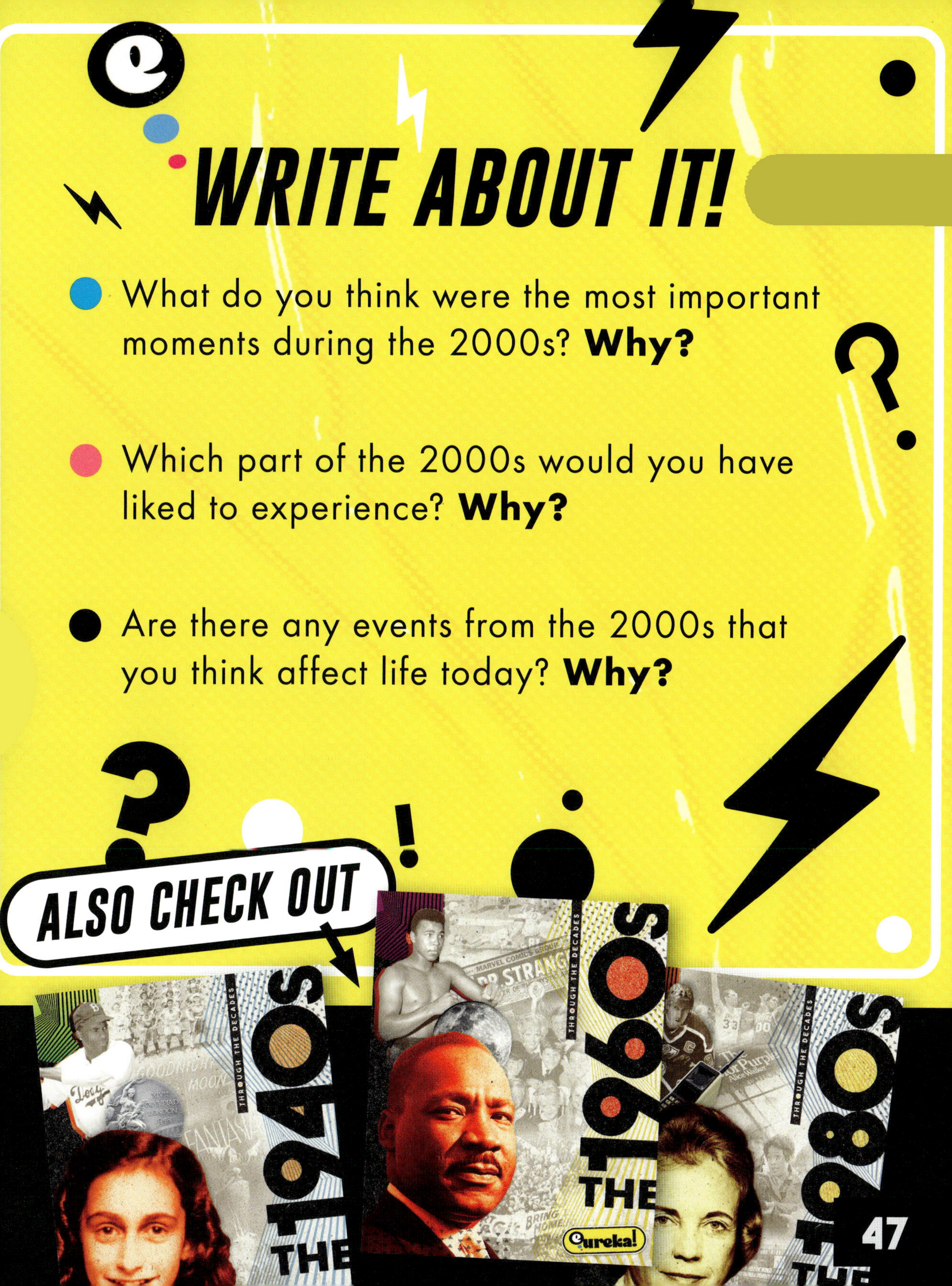

WRITE ABOUT IT!

- What do you think were the most important moments during the 2000s? **Why?**
- Which part of the 2000s would you have liked to experience? **Why?**
- Are there any events from the 2000s that you think affect life today? **Why?**

ALSO CHECK OUT

INDEX

The images in this book are reproduced through the courtesy of: Everett Collection, front cover (Obama), p. 45 (Obama); Dotted Yeti, front cover (Pluto), p. 22 (bottom); UPI/ Alamy Stock Photo, front cover (Brady), pp. 14 (top), 19 (Heller), 39 (bottom); Chronus/ Wikipedia, front cover (9/11); Rokas Tenys/ Alamy Stock Photo, front cover (The Office); CBW/ Alamy Stock Photo, front cover (Hunger Games); PA Images/ Alamy Stock Photo, front cover (Phelps), pp. 28 (Bratz), 37 (Beyoncé, The Black Eyed Peas); Getty Images/ Staff/ Getty Images, pp. 3 (9/11, Bin Laden), 8 (top), 13; marleyPug, pp. 3 (iPhone), 20; Tribune Content Agency LLC/ Alamy Stock Photo, pp. 3 (Tom Brady), 38 (Tom Brady); The Sims, p. 4 (Sims); oasisamuel, p. 4 (iPod nano); Ardy Dwi Prayoga, p. 4 (Razr); Richard Levine/ Alamy Stock Photo, p. 5 (Hot Topic); Martin Battilana Photography/ Alamy Stock Photo, p. 5 (scooter); Trevor Mogg Archive/ Alamy Stock Photo, p. 6 (top); trekandshoot, p. 6 (bottom); Winai Tepsuttinun, p. 7 (gas); Photo Builder, p. 7 (NYT); Artiom Photo, p. 7 (milk); phive2015, p. 7 (bread); AlenKadr, p. 7 (Coke); Sage Ross, p. 8 (middle); Orlando Sentinel/ Contributor/ Getty Images, p. 8 (bottom); MediaNews Group/ Pasadena Star-News via Getty Images/ Contributor/ Getty Images, p. 9 (top); Chip Somodevilla/ Staff/ Getty Images, pp. 9 (bottom), 19 (border patrol); Brooks Kraft/ Contributor/ Getty Images, pp. 10, 11 (Roberts); LUKE FRAZZA/ Staff/ Getty Images, p. 11 (Gore); Bloomberg/ Contributor/ Getty Images, p. 11 (Pelosi); Salma Bashir, p. 11 (Obama); Spencer Platt/ Staff/ Getty Images, p. 12 (top); Alex Wong/ Staff/ Gety Images, p. 12 (middle); Allan Tannenbaum/ Contributor/ Getty Images, p. 12 (bottom); DPLA/ Wikipedia, p. 13 (Bush); Peter Treanor/ Alamy Stock Photo, p. 14 (middle); RomanR, p. 14 (bottom); Historic Collection/ Alamy Stock Photo, p. 15 (Chávez); US Army Photo/ Alamy Stock Photo, p. 15 (Iraq War); MAHMUD HAMS/ Contributor/ Getty Images, p. 15 (Palestine); Dinodia Photos/ Alamy Stock Photo, p. 17 (top); Frans Delian, p. 17 (bottom); Michael Springer/ Stringer/ Getty Images, p. 18; David S. Holloway/ Contributor/ Getty Images, p. 19 (protest); Boston Globe/ Contributor/, p. 19 (Massachusetts); Hohum/ Wikipedia, p. 21 (Kindle); Donaldson Collection/ Contributor/ Getty Images, p. 21 (Nokia); Jeppe Gustafsson, p. 21 (social media); Ian Shaw/ Alamy Stock Photo, p. 21 (texting); Billion Photos, p. 22 (top); Newscast/ Contributor/ Getty Images, p. 22 (middle); Mike Peel/ Wikipedia, p. 23 (top); Belish, p. 23 (bottom); Hum Images/ Alamy Stock Photo, p. 24 (top); S.Candide, p. 24 (middle); TomBham/ Alamy Stock Photo, p. 24 (bottom); Karl Prouse/ Catwalking/ Contributor/ Getty Images, p. 26; Matryoha, p. 27 (boots); samuel wordley/ Alamy Stock Photo, p. 27 (Heelys); Dee Browning, p. 27 (necklace); Johnny Nunez/ Contributor/ Getty Images, p. 27 (tracksuit); PYMCA/ Avalon/ Contributor/ Getty Images, p. 27 (emo fashion); Robert Dant/ Alamy Stock Photo, p. 28 (Silly Bandz); Yamaguchi Haruyoshi/ Contributor/ Getty Images, p. 28 (dog); Rijal Jauhari Syahrulloh, p. 28 (Beyblade); ArcadeImages/ Alamy Stock Photo, p. 28 (Tony Hawk); robtek, p. 28 (PS2); Vitor Lando, p. 28 (Xbox 360); Tim O'Brien/ Wikipedia, p. 30; Retromags/ Wikipedia, p. 31 (Nintendo Power); John Reaves/ Wikipedia, p. 31 (Harry Potter); Malo/ Wikipedia, p. 31 (Artemis Fowl); Neopets, p. 31 (Neopets); Pictorial Press Ltd/ Alamy Stock Photo, pp. 32 (left), 33 (Jack Sparrow); United Archives GmbH/ Alamy Stock Photo, pp. 32 (right), 33 (Spider-Man); TCD/ Prod.DB/ Alamy Stock Photo, p. 33 (Gollum); Moviestore Collection Ltd/ Alamy Stock Photo, p. 33 (Polar Express); AJ Pics/ Alamy Stock Photo, pp. 34 (Grey's Anatomy), 35 (Spongebob Squarepants, That's So Raven); PictureLux/ The Hollywood Archive/ Alamy Stock Photo, pp. 34 (Survivor), 35 (The Office); AFF/ Alamy Stock Photo, p. 36; ZUMA Press, Inc./ Alamy Stock Photo, p. 37 (Daft Punk); dpa picture alliance archive/ Alamy Stock Photo, p. 37 (Fall Out Boy); Goddard Archive/ Alamy Stock Photo, p. 39 (top); David A Litman, p. 40 (Salt Lake City); MikeDotta, p. 40 (Turin); Pietro Basilico, p. 40 (Athens); Mark Green, p. 40 (Beijing); Regien Paassen, p. 40 (Sydney); Allstar Picture Library Ltd/ Alamy Stock Photo, p. 41 (Messi, Ronaldo); Independent/ Alamy Stock Photo, p. 41 (Williams); PCN Photography/ Alamy Stock Photo, p. 41 (Bolt); Abaca Press/ Alamy Stock Photo, p. 41 (Phelps); American Idol, p. 42 (American Idol); julie deshaies, p. 42 (Xbox); Michael Ventura/ Alamy Stock Photo, p. 43 (Human Genome Project); Ron Vesely/ Contributor/ Getty Images, p. 43 (Red Sox); Youtube, p. 43 (Youtube); Taylor Swift/ Wikipedia, p. 44 (Taylor Swift); seeshooteatrepeat, p. 44 (Wii); Maximum Film/ Alamy Stock Photo, p. 45 (Avatar).